THE AUTHOR

Leslie Blake: LLM, Barrister, Lecturer in Law at Surrey University. Leslie Blake is a partner of Environmental Training Consultants. In addition to his extensive experience as a lecturer and trainer he has regularly written articles in legal journals.

Rosalind Malcolm: LLB, Barrister, Lecturer in Law at Surrey University. She practises in Property, Trusts and Environmental Law as well as in Public Law. Rosalind Malcolm is currently conducting research into environmental impact assessment.

John Pointing: BA, MPhil, Barrister, now practises in chambers and is a partner of Environmental Training Consultants. He is the editor of *Alternatives to Custody,* 1986, published by Blackwell, and co-editor, with Mike Maguire, of *Victims of Crime: A New Deal?*, published in 1988 by Open University Press.

ENVIRONMENTAL TRAINING CONSULTANTS was set up in 1990 by a group of lawyers and environmental health professionals to develop legal training. Our aim is to work in very practical ways with people in local authorities, health authorities, professional organisations and industry to develop knowledge and expertise in the legal field.

CONTENTS

CHAPTER ONE:

INTRODUCTION

Prosecuting Food Safety Act Offences has developed from a series of training seminars concerned with food law prosecution, which the authors have undertaken with Environmental Health Officers. The seminars were organised by Environmental Training Consultants in conjunction with the Institution of Environmental Health Officers and were designed to assist EHOs responsible for implementing the 1990 Food Safety Act.

This book comprises a concise guide to food law and related legal issues. Although written specifically for environmental health professionals and students, it will also be a useful introduction to lawyers unfamiliar with this field. For a comprehensive analysis of food law, reference should be made to the standard reference works. These do not provide a comprehensive analysis of all aspects of law which EHOs require and little is to be found on procedure and evidence. Each particular case requires its own legal analysis and *Prosecuting Food Safety Act Offences* should not be seen as a substitute for taking legal advice.

One important issue we have found as trainers is the need for EHOs and their legal advisers to work closely together to minimise the risks of cases being lost when they reach court. This suggests that EHOs should give close attention to evidential matters at every stage of enquiry into an alleged food law offence. Although not intended to be a substitute for taking legal advice, this book should assist EHOs preparing their cases at all stages of the prosecution process. Furthermore, as key participants in a legal process, EHOs have to understand issues from the legal and, in effect, from the lawyer's point of view.

Broadly, three areas are covered in this booklet. Firstly, the main provisions of the Food Safety Act are outlined in Chapter 2. The criteria to be applied in bringing a prosecution are considered here and an analysis of the due diligence defence is provided. Particular attention has been given to this since a defended case will often be based on some aspect of due diligence and our experience is that EHOs have problems with this area.

Enforcement procedures are considered in Chapter 3, which includes discussion of the power to issue formal cautions. This chapter is divided according to the particular section in the Act. This has been done not only because the subject matter and powers available are organised by section, but also because such procedures as the rules for serving notices vary. This chapter draws extensively on the Codes of Practice issued under s.40 of the Food Safety Act.

Evidential matters are considered in Chapter 4. The law of evidence, particularly in criminal proceedings, is a highly complicated area for practitioners and academic lawyers alike. We have written a concise account of the various types of evidence, including hearsay evidence. The rules of hearsay produce difficulties and confusion for anyone wishing to understand legal matters. Accordingly, we have written a concise, practical guide which we believe EHOs will find helpful.

A full analysis of procedural matters is beyond the scope of this booklet. It is, however, important that EHOs understand the rules for giving evidence in court, the rights which suspects have under common law and the Police and Criminal Evidence Act 1984, and the restrictions on the use of previous warnings and convictions in current proceedings. Chapter 4 also considers pleas in mitigation and costs.

Whilst the use of particular words and phrases is essential in any legal discourse, in writing this book we have attempted to avoid the use of jargon. This should allow the interested lay person to understand the material and also the difficulties faced by those having to implement the legislation. Members of the public also have the right to know what actions are, or should be, carried out by EHOs acting on their behalf. In accordance with legal convention, the masculine pronoun has been used in the book.

CHAPTER TWO:

THE FOOD SAFETY ACT 1990

The Act provides a new framework for enforcing food hygiene requirements and for controlling food manufacture and distribution systems. Because it is new there are as yet few precedents on interpretation. Certain aspects, such as the mechanisms for enforcement governed by improvement and prohibition notice procedures, are familiar from other areas of law, for example health and safety.

The Act is intended to simplify prosecutions. Guidelines for enforcement are provided in various Codes of Practice issued under s.40. Many of the Food Regulations issued under older legislation remain in force for the time being.

The Act was substantially in force by 1 January 1991; and completely so from 3 April 1992.

The main intentions of the Act are:-

● To give a higher priority to food safety in the wake of increased public anxieties and media concern with regard to international contamination (e.g. Chernobyl), food terrorism (e.g. glass fragments in baby food), and increases in serious food poisoning cases;

● To consolidate previous legislation and make UK food law more consistent with EC law;

● To increase the penalties for violations and to strengthen enforcement powers;

● To encourage greater uniformity between authorities responsible for administering the Act.

The Act has been broadly welcomed, although initially there were fears in the food industry about the extensive powers available to ministers to make regulations. There have also been concerns about enforcement responsibilities being shared between non-metropolitan district and county councils rather than being consolidated under a unitary authority. More recently, EHOs have been exposed to criticism in the media for adopting an "over-zealous" approach, and it seems likely that the relevant Codes of Practice on enforcement will be reformed. There is also widespread recognition that many of the Food Regulations require updating.

Codes of Practice

The power to issue Codes of Practice conferred by s.40 has been extensively used. There are currently 14 Codes in operation:-

1. Responsibility for Enforcement of the Food Safety Act 1990.
2. Legal Matters.
3. Inspection Procedures - General.
4. Inspection, Detention and Seizure of Food.

5.   The Use of Improvement Notices.
6.   Prohibition Procedures.
7.   Sampling for Analysis or Examination.
8.   Food Standards Inspections.
9.   Food Hygiene Inspections.
10. Enforcement of the Temperature Control Requirements of Food Hygiene Regulations.
11. Enforcement of the Food Premises (Registration) Regulations.
12. Division of Enforcement Responsibilities for the Quick Frozen Foodstuffs Regulations 1990.
13. Enforcement of the Food Safety Act 1990 in relation to Crown Premises.
16. Enforcement of the Food Safety Act 1990 in relation to the Food Hazard Warning System.

Section 40 of the Act says that food authorities **must** have regard to those parts of the Codes specified in bold in the text and **should** have regard to the remaining parts. These requirements fall short of compelling food authorities slavishly to follow the Codes, but they should comply unless there is a genuine reason not to. Failure to comply is unlikely to be fatal to a prosecution unless it results in unfairness to the defendant.

Food Safety Act Prosecution

As with other areas of criminal law, to obtain a conviction it is normally necessary for a prosecutor to prove all the elements of an alleged food law offence. The burden of proof on the prosecutor is to prove any such offence to the criminal standard, i.e. "beyond reasonable doubt". Where the defendant pleads a due diligence defence, the burden on him is "on the balance of probabilities".

The Decision to Prosecute

The local authority always has a discretion whether or not to prosecute an offence. Public policy considerations as well as such matters as degree of culpability, prevalence, seriousness and frequency are all relevant to such a decision. Code of Practice No.2: lists various factors the local authority should consider when deciding to prosecute. These are:-

● Seriousness

● Previous history of the party concerned

● Likelihood of establishing a due diligence defence

● Ability of any important witnesses and their willingness to cooperate

● Willingness of the party to prevent recurrences

● Probable public benefit of prosecution and importance of the case

● Whether a caution or improvement notice might have been more effective or appropriate

● Any explanation offered by the affected company.

The decision to prosecute can be and often is delegated to any authorised member or officer of the local authority under s.223 Local Government Act 1972. The Code of Practice factors listed above will apply to any EHO having delegated authority to prosecute. If the decision is made by the council it should not be made in open session, since this could prejudice the case against the accused. Deciding whether to prosecute should be based on the merits of the case and not be influenced by political considerations. It is legitimate to implement a prosecution policy to "blitz" alleged offenders, provided that the Code of Practice factors outlined above are fully considered.

Particular Offences Under the Food Safety Act
A majority of prosecutions are taken under the Food Hygiene Regulations. Where an alleged offence is being prosecuted under the Food Safety Act, the Code recommends using s.7 or s.8 wherever possible rather than s.14.

Section 7 - Rendering food injurious to health
Section 7 is derived from early legislation to combat food adulteration. Nowadays, direct adulteration is quite rare, and similar provisions in previous legislation (s.1 Food Act 1984) were rarely used.

This section applies to any person who renders food injurious to health by:-

a)   adding any article or substance, or
b)   using any article or substance as an ingredient in the preparation of the food, or
c)   abstracting any constituent from the food, or
d)   subjecting the food to any other process or treatment,
      with intent that it will be sold for human consumption.

Consideration of whether any of the prescribed acts is injurious to the health can include the probable cumulative effects of consumption, in ordinary quantities.

Section 8 - Selling food not complying with the food safety requirements
Section 8 makes it an offence to sell food breaching the food safety requirements, which is defined as food:-

a)   rendered injurious to health by section 7, or
b)   unfit for human consumption, or
c)   so contaminated that it would not be reasonable to expect it to be used for human consumption.

Liability encompasses not only the actual selling or possession for sale of food. It includes situations where one "offers, exposes or advertises" food for sale for human consumption, or where one possesses or passes to another food in preparation for such a sale. It follows, therefore, that offences can take place in premises other than retail outlets and that a range of acts beyond actual selling may be illegal.

Section 8 provides that where food fails the food safety requirements, all food of the same class or description in a batch, lot or consignment is deemed to fail. Thus it is up to the defendant to show why the remainder should not fail.

Sections 14 and 15 - Consumer protection
Consumer protection is incorporated into the Act by s.14 and s.15. Section 14 makes it an offence to sell to the purchaser's prejudice any food which is not of the nature or substance or quality demanded. Section 15 applies to the false description or advertising of food, including providing misleading information.

Division of Responsibilities
Responsibility for the enforcement of the Act is with the London boroughs, district authorities and non-metropolitan counties. In parts of the country where there are no unified authorities, both county councils and district councils may take legal proceedings under sections 7, 8 and 14 of the Act. In these areas, each district and county council should designate a specific liaison officer. A co-ordinating group should be set up to co-ordinate information and procedures.

Section 5(4) allows Ministers to assign responsibilities to a particular tier of local government. The following division of responsibilities is stipulated in Code of Practice No.1:

1) District councils: contamination by micro-organisms; mould or physical contaminants in food;
2) County councils: chemical contamination; compositional offences, adulteration, misleading claims.

This is not a rigid division. Where there is an imminent risk to health from chemical contamination, the Code stipulates that district councils should be responsible for the investigation and any subsequent prosecution. Regulations made or deemed to be made under the Food Safety Act specify the level of local government responsible for their enforcement.

Penalties
Section 35 of the Act provides for increased fines for food law convictions: up to £20,000 per count for the main offences. Except for obstruction - which is summary only, incurring a maximum sentence of a £5,000 fine (level 5) and/or 3 months prison - all other offences are triable either in the Magistrates' Court or Crown Court. Magistrates' increased powers to fine serious cases should mean that only exceptionally will prosecutions take place in the Crown Court.

Convictions in the Crown Court incur a maximum sentence of an unlimited fine and/or 2 years prison. Convictions under sections 7, 8 and 14 in the Magistrates' Court attract maximum sentences of £20,000 and/or 6 months prison. The maximum for other Food Safety Act offences is £5,000 and/or 6 months prison.

Due Diligence Defence

An important defence is provided under s.21 of the Food Safety Act, namely the statutory defence of due diligence. Its purpose is partly to mitigate the harshness that might result from convicting a person who unwittingly commits a strict liability offence. This defence is also available to ensure that those parties truly responsible for the offence are the ones prosecuted.

Section 21 provides that it is a defence: "for the person charged to prove that he took all reasonable precautions and exercised all due diligence to avoid the commission of the offence by himself or by a person under his control".

The burden of proof is on the defendant, who has to prove his defence on the balance of probabilities. Under s.21(5), a person relying on a due diligence defence who alleges that the offence was due to the act or default of another, or that he relied on information supplied by another, must give the court:-

a)   at least 7 clear days notice before the hearing; and
b)   where he has previously appeared before a court in connection with the alleged offence, within one month of his first appearance, he must serve a written notice on the prosecutor identifying that other person.

These requirements can only be waived with the leave of the court. Their intention is to prevent the defence from springing a surprise on the prosecution.

Section 21(2) modifies full due diligence requirements with regard to persons charged under sections 8, 14 or 15 of the Act who neither:-

a)   prepared the food in question, nor
b)   imported it into Great Britain.

In practice, s.21(2) applies to retailers who do not prepare the food, though wholesalers or others not preparing or importing food would be covered also. A retailer has a complete due diligence defence provided he proves that the offence was due to the act or default of another person not under his control, or, that the offence was due to his reliance on information supplied by that person. Note that an employer cannot rely on this part of the defence if the act or default was committed by his employee.

Section 21(3) provides a further requirement to the "own brander", who must show that any reasonable checks were carried out by him, or that it was reasonable for him to rely on any checks carried out by the supplier. The intention here is to ensure that someone in the production/distribution chain carried out all checks that were reasonable in the circumstances. The "own brander" also has to prove that he did not know and had no reason to suspect that his act or omission would amount to an offence.

Other retailers have a slightly less onerous burden. Under s.21(4) they have to show that they did not know, and could not reasonably be expected to have known at the time of the offence, that their act or omission constituted an offence.

General Principles of Due Diligence

The availability of a due diligence defence imposes a higher standard on the food industry than previously and replaces the "written warranty" defence contained in the Food Act 1984. The Food Safety Act applies to every stage of the production and distribution process, from farmers to processors to retailers. However, it should be noted that the provisions in s.21(3) and (4), regarding retailers' reliance on information supplied by another, give them a form of qualified warranty protection similar to that formerly available under s.102 Food Act 1984.

What is encapsulated in the due diligence defence is what is reasonable in the circumstances. In other words, what is important depends on the facts of a particular case rather than on some fixed formula or standard. The legislative intention was for standards of monitoring, checking and control to be raised. It is arguable whether the courts give adequate recognition to this aim.

Judicial interpretation of due diligence in relation to the Food Safety Act is as yet largely unexplored. However, there are many cases based on the old food law and on other legislation such as consumer safety and trade descriptions. These only provide us with general principles concerning due diligence, but not ones specific to the Act. The following principles are relevant to food law:-

- Due diligence is a question of fact; it is for the magistrates (or jury in exceptional cases prosecuted in the Crown Courts) to decide whether a defendant has discharged his burden of proof.

- The burden of proof is on the defendant; therefore the standard for discharging it is the balance of probabilities.

- Every case depends on its own circumstances; there is no standard system of due diligence. It follows that codes of practice can only serve as guides to fulfil the requirements of a due diligence system:
    "To lay down general tests of law in the absence of full arguments is, in general, undesirable when the test ought to be applied to an ever changing situation and where the subject matter of the test is the question whether or not reasonable precautions have been taken and due diligence exercised" (Lord Justice Parker in *Zawadski v Sleigh* [1975]).
    This judgment, taken from a case brought under the Trade Descriptions Act, suggests that nothing should be assumed or taken to be self-evident in preparing a prosecution where due diligence is likely to be relied upon.

- Defendants must take all reasonable precautions. A due diligence system must be comprehensive, involving **all** not merely some reasonable precautions. This implies taking any reasonable precautions that could be taken. What is reasonable depends not only on what the defendant actually did, but also on such factors as the size and resources of his business.

- The system of due diligence must include adequate checks that are systematically recorded, and staff must be provided with adequate instructions and training. Without such measures a business may be unable to prove it took all reasonable precautions.

- A sufficient number of tests must be carried out in a system of control, and the results of such tests reported and considered. Tests should also be carried out in a proper manner.

- Lack of expert knowledge is no defence in the sense that being a non-expert does not absolve a person from taking reasonable steps and exercising due diligence.

- A blanket assurance from a supplier is not enough. It may only be reasonable to rely on a specific assurance given in relation to particular goods.

- The precautions to be taken must be reasonable bearing in mind the nature of the operation. In other words, it would not be reasonable to expect perfection, or measures to be taken involving considerable cost for small benefit.

- Due diligence must be exercised by the "directing mind" - the person or persons who control the company. This principle does not prevent the responsibility for administering a due diligence system being delegated to an employee or agent. Whether such delegation provides a defence to those who control a company depends on the circumstances, including the size and organisation of the business.

- Default of staff within a due diligence system. The responsibilities of a company with many shops or other units is limited to devising a proper system to ensure compliance with the law and to setting up proper arrangements for checking that system. Provided these conditions are adhered to, any food law offences committed by employees will not involve the additional liability of the company or those controlling it.

In general, a due diligence system must be effective and sufficient to deal with foreseeable problems; and be capable of preventing faults and correcting those that do occur. Perfection is not a requirement, but positive action to do all that could reasonably be expected to be done is. The system must cover all aspects of the business subject to the Food Safety Act and the Food Regulations, including:-

- Hygiene and safety of premises and equipment;

- Quality, composition and safety of food products;

- Labelling and advertising;

- Staff training;

- Where applicable, registration and licensing requirements, improvement notices, prohibition or control orders.

Demands for modifications to be made involving disproportionate cost, where the risk to health or likelihood of injury is small, are unlikely to be found reasonable in court. The risk of injury will be highly relevant however - particularly serious injury and where the risk was, or should have been, obvious. Normal or average trade practices - even where these fall below the high standards EHOs try to encourage - can be very influential with magistrates. The size and organisation of the firm are likely to be highly relevant in deciding on the adequacy of a due diligence system. In general, wisdom after the event will be a poor persuader in court that a defendant acted unreasonably.

It is important to appreciate that we have been considering general principles which have yet to be tested in the higher courts in relation to the Food Safety Act. Despite the legislative intention in the Act to encourage higher standards backed by increased codification, a sense of realism and proportion is essential in assessing what a court is likely to accept as reasonable.

CHAPTER THREE:

POWERS OF ENFORCEMENT

Formal Cautions

In certain cases, a formal caution can be issued as an alternative to prosecution. The Local Authority Co-ordinating Body on Food and Trading Standards [LACOTS] has provided specimen documentation [Food Safety circular FS2 92 3 of 27 April 1992] based on general procedures set down in Home Office circular 59/1990.

A formal caution requires there to be:

1) sufficient evidence of the offender's guilt to make conviction a realistic prospect; and
2) an admission of guilt; and
3) such understanding of its significance as to enable the offender to give his informed consent to the caution.

The decision whether to issue a formal caution should be guided by such factors as the nature and seriousness of the offence, the likely penalty, the offender's age and state of health, his previous offence history and attitude to the offence for which a formal caution is contemplated.

The formal caution, issued according to Home Office procedures, can be cited in court in any subsequent offence for which the person is found guilty. Consequently, it can be taken into account when deciding penalty. Details of cautions should be recorded and sent to the Central Register of Convictions operated by the Office of Fair Trading.

Section 9 Powers: Inspection, Detention and Seizure of Food

Where an officer believes that food does not comply with the food safety requirements, or is likely to cause food poisoning or a disease communicable to human beings, then he has the power to inspect the food and to seize it. The officer's powers are governed by s.9.

The powers of inspection, detention and seizure of food are sufficiently wide to extend to all situations occurring between production and distribution. The officer may inspect at any stage in the process. The first stage is the inspection. If, on inspection, it appears to the officer that the food fails to comply with the food safety requirements as defined in s.8, he may exercise the powers conferred by s.9. Where the food is likely to cause food poisoning or any disease communicable to human beings, then these powers are available even when there is no inspection. Food poisoning is not defined in the Act. However, it is likely to be given a wide interpretation and a Code of Practice is expected on this point.

When Can Powers be Used?

Section 9 powers can be exercised "at all reasonable times". This certainly includes shop opening hours. However, an officer may conclude that because of the dangerous nature of the food, an inspection should take place before the shop next opens - over the weekend, for example. Under the previous legislation it was thought that reasonable times were limited to opening hours. What is reasonable is a factual question, which depends on the particular circumstances. If it is essential to inspect food swiftly, then the courts may well accept the argument that to require a manager to open up the shop on a Sunday was perfectly reasonable.

These powers apply to food which is intended for human consumption and is subject to the process of sale. Any items that are commonly used in the preparation of food and kept on the premises where food is sold will be presumed to be for human consumption. So, if the owner of the premises argues that some product which is normally used for human consumption is not going to end up being eaten, then he must establish that fact, on a balance of probabilities, to the court's satisfaction.

Definitions

The "process of sale" includes situations where the food:-

a)   has been sold or is offered or exposed for sale; or
b)   is in the possession of, or has been deposited with or consigned to, any person for the purposes of sale or of preparation for sale.

The expression "offer for sale" is derived from contract law. An offer for sale is that stage in a transaction which requires only acceptance for the contract to be concluded. Goods displayed in a self-service store or in the window of a shop are not technically being offered for sale. The legal status of such goods is as an "invitation to treat". When the shopper approaches the cash desk and offers to buy the goods, that is the offer which can be accepted or rejected by the vendor.

"Exposure for sale" includes goods that are unsold at the end of the day and are returned to the depot - the unsold milk on a milk float, for example.

"Possession" for the purposes of sale has, in general, been given its popular meaning. Physical possession is implied. It must be possession for the purposes of sale. If it has been set aside then it may not be covered by this section. The important point is to observe whether the items have been separated from others being used in the preparation of food.

If the food has been transferred to another person for some process to take place - where, for example, the frozen food industry sends fresh peas to be frozen and then receives them back for sale - this will be covered by the expression "deposited with".

"Consigned to" covers the transfer of the food to some other person for the purpose of dispatching it onwards.

Inspection Procedures

Inspection procedures are laid out in the Code of Practice No.3: "Inspection Procedures - General". Inspection means a visit to any food premises to inspect the premises, equipment, processes, personnel, food, labels, or records. In addition, there are two detailed Codes which should be consulted: Code of Practice No.8: "Food Standards Inspections", and Code of Practice No.9: "Food Hygiene Inspections". Sampling and analysis may then take place in accordance with the Food Safety (Sampling and Qualifications) Regulations 1990 and Code of Practice No.7: "Sampling for Analysis or Examination".

There is no need to give notice before the inspection: the element of surprise may be useful. If there is more than one food authority involved, or more than one enforcement authority, then the inspection visits should be co-ordinated. Failure to adopt a co-ordinated approach is likely to lose the prosecution the sympathy of the court. Officers should only carry out inspections outside their own area where this is necessary to investigate offences occurring within their area. They should give the other authority advance notification.

Post-Inspection Procedures

After the inspection, the officer should give a written report to the person carrying on the business. The report should state the date, time and place of the inspection, what was examined, whether any samples were taken and the conclusions. If in the officer's view there has been a contravention, then the report may take the form of a formal notice, for example, an improvement notice. Once this stage has been cleared the officer has a choice: to serve a notice restricting the use and movement of the food, or to seize it.

Service of a Detention or Seizure Notice

A notice is served on the person in charge of the food; and should be in the form specified in the Prescribed Forms Regulations. It should be delivered or sent to that person at their usual or last known address, or to the secretary or clerk at the company's registered office. Normally, the notice should be served by hand; then there is no doubt about whether it was received.

The owner of the food should also be notified of the service of the notice; this could be done, for example, by fax. This is necessary because anyone who might be liable to prosecution under s.7 and s.8 has a right to be heard in the court proceedings. If reasonable enquiries have failed to ascertain the name and address of the proprietor of the food business, then the notice should be sent to the "owner" (or "occupier") of the premises; and should either be delivered to some person on the premises or fixed to the premises in a conspicuous position.

Detain or Seize?

A detention of food notice may be served when an authorised officer has good reason to suspect that the food does not satisfy the food safety requirements. The purpose of the notice is to ensure that the food is not used for human consumption and is either held where it is, or not moved except to a specified place pending further enquiries (food analysis, for example). The notice should be signed by, or on behalf of, the officer taking the decision to detain. If the officer already has evidence about the food, then it should be seized and a notice warning of the intention to apply for condemnation may be served.

The decision to detain should be carefully weighed in the light of such factors as the possible financial implications to the industry or to the authority. Compensation may well be payable if the grounds for removing the food prove to be insufficient to support the action. Guidance on this point is given in the Code of Practice No.4: "Inspection, Detention and Seizure of Suspect Food". Such matters as the perishable nature of the food, or its physical security, should be taken into account in deciding where it should be kept. Clearly, the officer needs to act promptly and to consult the owner or person in charge of the food whenever possible. As to who should bear the cost, the Code suggests that this depends on who is requiring the food to be moved. If it is the officer, the authority bears the cost; otherwise it is the owner.

Seizure of Food

When it has been decided to seize the food, it is essential that the officer is able to prove that the food seized is the same as that which is produced in court. For such evidential purposes, the officer should ensure that the food is not left unattended. Wherever the food is stored, the officer must be confident that it will not be moved, used for human consumption, or destroyed. Food which has been detained should be tested within 21 days, or sooner if possible.

The officer should act immediately the evidence has been obtained. A withdrawal of detention of food notice should be served - as soon as possible - if there is no evidence of a breach. Otherwise, the food should be seized and a notice served warning of the intention to apply for condemnation.

If the food in breach of the requirements is part of a lot, there is a rebuttable presumption that the whole lot is in breach. Where the officer has serious doubts about the state of the rest of the food then he should consider seizing the whole lot.

Obstruction

It is an offence under s.33 Food Safety Act to refuse entry to an officer; and a person committing this offence should be cautioned. The officer may be accompanied by the police and any other necessary person, such as a food examiner. Where necessary, an entry warrant under s.32(2) can be obtained, which must be exercised within one month. Difficulties over entry or inspection are generally resolved by the presence of a constable and the police are usually willing to assist other enforcement officers. The police are also under a duty to avoid breaches of the peace. A person commits an offence if he contravenes a notice of detention or other notice under s.9 of the Act, provided that he either knew what he was doing or wilfully shut his eyes to the contravention.

Compensation

Compensation is payable where a detention notice is withdrawn or if a Justice of the Peace refuses to condemn the food. It is desirable, therefore, that at the time of seizure the owner and officer agree the following matters:-

● the date of manufacture of the food

● its declared shelf life

● the age of the food at the time of detention

● the quantity of food

● conditions of storage required

● the value of the food as paid by the owner.

This information should preclude potential arguments about the amount of compensation payable.

Bringing the Case to Court

The best approach for the newcomer to a court is to establish contact with the clerk and to become familiar with the way the local court operates. When action in respect of a detention notice is contemplated, telephone the court and find out when a Justice of the Peace will be available. Ask what information the JP is likely to require concerning the food and use this when completing the food condemnation warning notice and the notice to be served. The court will sit outside normal court hours (between 10 a.m. and 4 p.m.). It is important to keep the goodwill of the court, so it is advisable to seek a hearing outside normal hours only in an emergency.

The officer who served the notice should be the one to appear in court. If that is not possible then another officer can appear, but he must be fully briefed. This is particularly important if a solicitor is representing the authority. Destruction of the food is normally the best order to seek. This ensures that the food does not end up back on the market. The owner pays the cost of destruction or disposal; the authority bears the responsibility for organising the disposal.

Section 10 Powers: Improvement Notices

Where an officer has reasonable grounds for believing that the proprietor of a food business has failed to comply with the regulations, an improvement notice may be served requiring him to remedy the defect. The officer's powers are governed by s.10. The relevant regulations are listed in Code of Practice No.6: "Prohibition Procedures".

Unlike an informal letter or warning, improvement notices have statutory force and, therefore, attract a penalty if they are ignored. The penalty is up to £5,000 or imprisonment for a maximum of six months, on summary conviction. On indictment, the penalty is an unlimited fine and/or imprisonment for up to two years.

When to Use Powers

An improvement notice should only be served when an authorised officer is satisfied that there has been a contravention of one of the relevant food hygiene or food processing regulations **and** where this does not pose an imminent risk to health. Informal procedures - giving oral advice, sending advisory letters and informal warnings - can still be used, but only if such procedures are believed to be as effective as statutory ones in obtaining compliance. Code of Practice No.5: "The Use of Improvement Notices" stipulates that the notice procedure should be considered as the first option. The Code also states that enforcement authorities should avoid adopting the policy of issuing notices after informal procedures have failed.

The Code has been criticised because its practical effect is to discourage the use of informal procedures to obtain compliance with the regulations. Replacement of informal methods by the notice procedure would constitute a significant loss in the enforcement process. Such a result would not appear to be the intention behind the Code, but the use of informal letters is implicitly discouraged.

The notice should only be served once the officer has sufficient information and evidence to substantiate a case should there be an appeal. In addition, the Code urges that great care should be taken to ensure that the notice is correctly drawn, since a procedural or technical fault will defeat the proceedings. The problem requiring action should be clearly identified in the notice so that the person responsible is left in no doubt as to the remedy. A notice can be served whether or not the authority is considering prosecution for the breach of the regulations.

Who Should Serve the Notice?

The notice should be served only by a fully qualified officer with experience in food law enforcement. These are EHOs enforcing food hygiene or food processing regulations and official veterinary surgeons, designated under the Fresh Meat Export (Hygiene and Inspection) Regulations 1987 and carrying out official veterinary surgeon duties. There was some criticism of the improvement notice procedure when it was first introduced in that it empowered officers to make quasi-judicial decisions in circumstances where there was no provision for compensation. The requirement in the Code, indicating that only senior and experienced officers will be able to serve these notices, is an attempt to reassure the food industry that notices will be used with consistency and discrimination.

On Whom to Serve the Notice

The notice should be served on the proprietor. Under s.53(1) of the Act, this is defined as the person "by whom a food business is carried out". The term "food business" is a broad one and the notice procedure can be utilised at different levels in the business. In addition, the person who is to carry out the remedial work, such as the local manager, receives a copy.

Where it is not possible to locate the proprietor, undue delay in serving the notice should be avoided. If the identity of the proprietor cannot be discovered, then the notice should be addressed to and served on the "owner" and left on the premises.

Such a course of action is a last resort; all steps should have been taken to trace the actual owner first (e.g. searches of the register of food premises and company searches). The person who is apparently in charge should be asked who the proprietor is. Questions should be put to workers on the premises as to the name of their employer; the payroll could be checked. If there are language problems the officer should consider taking an interpreter. This will be a requirement if the officer wishes to take statements from people who have difficulties understanding English and who request an interpreter. Searches could also be made, for example, at H.M. Land Registry, the commercial rating register, and at the Driver Vehicle Licensing Centre for ownership of any vehicles observed on the premises.

How Should the Notice be Served?

Where possible, the notice should be served by hand, by a competent person who can explain what it means. If this is not possible, it can be served by first class post, and proof of posting and/or advice of delivery should be obtained. It can be faxed for speed, but this is not a legal service, so a fax must always be followed by a hard copy.

Drafting the Notice

The form of the notice is set out in the Food Safety (Prescribed Forms) Regulations 1991, (SI 1991 No. 100; 22 January 1991). In completing the form, it is essential that the breach is clearly specified. This means that the matters giving rise to the contravention should be spelled out and the legal basis for the notice made clear.

Time Limits

The time limit for remedying the defect must be a minimum of 14 days (not including the first day on which the notice is served). It is important for a reasonable and realistic time to be allowed in the notice, otherwise an appeal is likely to succeed. The Code states that the following factors should be taken into account:-

● the nature of the problem

● the risk to health

● the availability of solutions.

If the proprietor asks for an extension of the time limit on genuine grounds, the request should be considered sympathetically. The officer should consider the risk, the reason for the request, the remedy, the past record of co-operation of the proprietor and any interim measures proposed. The proprietor should be told that such requests must be made in writing before the period specified in the notice expires.

Work of Equivalent Effect

There is a provision in the form which states that the proprietor may undertake work having an equivalent effect. Although a right, a proprietor would be well advised to first discuss any alternative with the officer able to authorise it. This is because a failure to provide a satisfactory remedy as advised will not constitute compliance with the notice.

Appeals

There is a right of appeal to the Magistrates' Court against an improvement notice. An appeal must be brought within one month from the date of service or the period specified in the notice, whichever is the shorter. Until the appeal is heard the effect of the notice is suspended. The court may cancel, affirm or modify the notice on appeal. If it is dismissed by the magistrates, a further right of appeal lies to the Crown Court.

Completion of the Work

The officer should check the work as soon as notification is received that it is complete. It should ideally be checked by the officer who issued the notice. Details of the notice and its outcome should be recorded on the authority's register.

Sections 11 and 12: Prohibition Procedures

It may be necessary on public health grounds to close down premises, halt processes, stop the use of equipment, or to prevent an individual operating within the food industry. There are two procedures designed to achieve these ends - sections 11 and 12 of the Act. Both procedures are subject to court proceedings.

A prohibition order must be imposed by the court where it considers that the premises, equipment or process put public health at risk. The court may also, at its discretion, ban the proprietor or manager from managing a food business.

The officer may believe that there is an imminent risk of injury to health, which must be dealt with without the delay of making an application to the court. In this case an emergency prohibition notice may be served by the officer, which has the immediate effect of stopping the offending activity. An application to the court for an emergency prohibition order must then be made within three clear days, not including the date of service. Alternatively, an application to the court for an emergency prohibition order may be made without first serving an emergency prohibition notice.

In choosing the more appropriate procedure, the critical question for the officer is whether the risk of injury to health is imminent. Code of Practice No.6 provides guidance on the meaning of this term. For example, a high risk of food poisoning within the next few days would be sufficient. The Code states that it is the risk of injury which must be imminent; actual injury, such as injury to an unborn child, need not appear until later. Exposure to the risk of injury in such a case would be sufficient to take emergency action. Medical or other advice should be sought where the matter is specialised and requires an expert opinion.

The officer should take note of the question of compensation. If the emergency notice is not confirmed by the court then compensation may be payable.

S.11 Prohibition Orders
There are two conditions which must be satisfied before the court will grant a prohibition order:-

1) the proprietor is convicted of an offence under one of the Regulations; and,
2) the court which convicts the proprietor is satisfied that the health risk condition is fulfilled with respect to that business.

There are three situations which can constitute a risk of injury to health and which can, therefore, satisfy the health risk condition. These are:-

1) the use of any process or treatment;
2) the construction of premises for the business or the use of equipment; and,
3) the state or condition of the premises or equipment.

A prohibition order can be sought in relation to any one of these activities. In addition, an order can be sought banning the food business proprietor or the manager, from participating in the management of any food business. The manager is the person who is responsible for the day-to-day running of the business or any part of the business.

How to Apply for a Prohibition Order
The first step is to bring a prosecution for the contravention of one of the Regulations. It is for the officer to seek the prohibition order under s.11 once a conviction has been secured. The proprietor or representative should be warned, in writing or orally, of the intention to seek a prohibition order before the hearing. The proprietor should not be taken by surprise, so any evidence should be disclosed in advance.

It is highly desirable for the officer to attend court in person even when a guilty plea has been lodged. Further evidence may be necessary, or the court may require an opinion before granting a prohibition order. Evidence should be available as to the state of the premises or equipment at all relevant times. If a prohibition order is sought against a proprietor or manager, evidence of any previous convictions or warnings should be sought and presented to the court. The Office of Fair Trading should be contacted for this information. It is essential that every conviction and prohibition order is reported to the OFT, in sufficient detail, for other authorities to make use of this system effectively.

Service of the Order
The order should be served by hand. It is desirable to serve the order on the proprietor before leaving the court. Consultation with the Clerk to the Justices should enable the order to be swiftly drawn up and served. If there are partners, each partner should be served, although failure to do so does not invalidate the order.

S.12 Emergency Prohibition Notice
If the officer decides that the risk of injury to health is imminent then the procedure for issuing an emergency prohibition notice under s.12 is appropriate. The practice

in some local authorities is to require, where there is thought to be an imminent risk, that an inspection is undertaken by two authorised officers. Given the draconian nature of the s.12 notice, the adoption of such a practice should be seriously considered.

Service of the Notice

Only authorised officers may sign the notice. These officers should be fully qualified with experience in food law enforcement. Consideration should be given to establishing a duty system to ensure that an authorised officer is available at all times to issue a notice under this procedure.

It is preferable to serve the notice by hand. If not possible, then it can be served by post with proof of posting or advice of delivery. As additional evidence it is advisable for the officer to keep a record of the time of service. A copy of the notice must be fixed in a conspicuous place on the premises, such as the inside of the glass of a front window. The prohibition takes immediate effect: once the notice is served, not when it is received.

The notice can prohibit any of the activities set out in s.11, with the exception of a ban on a person. Only a court can impose such a ban.

Effects of Service

Once the notice has been served various courses of action can be taken. The notice may achieve its effect in that the risk to health is removed. On application by the proprietor, the authority may then issue a certificate to the effect that the health risk condition has been removed. The authority has 14 days in which to reply to such an application. If a certificate is granted it must be issued within three days of the decision.

The notice expires if, within three days of service, no application is made to the court for an emergency prohibition order. The period is counted from the first day after service of the notice. Where an application for an order is made, the notice remains in force until the application has been dealt with.

Emergency Prohibition Orders

If the notice is confirmed the court will make an emergency prohibition order. An alternative procedure is available where an officer decides not to serve a notice, but to seek an emergency prohibition order direct. In any event, the proprietor must receive one day's notice of the date of application for the order. If the application follows an emergency prohibition notice, then it will be convenient to serve notice of the court hearing at the same time as serving the notice itself.

Given the speed with which such an application to the court needs to be launched, it is essential to have procedures in place which have been agreed with the local authority legal department. Contact with the local court clerk and familiarity with the practices in the local court will ease the way when speed is essential.

Inspections should take place between the service of the notice and the court hearing. There may be a delay before the court can hear the case and it is important to monitor compliance with the notice. Periodic inspections may be undertaken by a different officer, but the final inspection, which should be on the day of the hearing or the day before, should be made by the authorised officer who initiated the action.

Service of the order follows the same procedure as for the prohibition order.

Appeals
Appeals against prohibition orders and emergency prohibition orders are made to the Crown Court.

Section 13: Emergency Control Orders

This order is designed to deal with health hazards which are not localised and cannot therefore be dealt with effectively by one authority acting alone. Under s.13 of the Act, the Minister may issue an emergency control order where any commercial operations relating to food, food sources or contact materials involve an imminent risk to health. The order may prohibit the carrying out of such operations.

Crown Premises

As from 1 April 1992, Crown premises have been subject to many of the provisions of the Food Safety Act. These may be inspected in the same way as privately run food businesses and officers may enter them to investigate complaints. Depending on the nature of the Crown premises - for example, whether they are a prison or a restaurant in a Royal park - different arrangements for inspection will need to be made. Guidelines are contained in Code of Practice No.13.

The Crown cannot be made criminally liable, but is otherwise subject to the enforcement process, including the issue of improvement notices. The local authority also has the power to make an application by originating summons to the High Court. The Court may make a declaration that the contravention is unlawful. This course of action is only likely to arise in the most exceptional circumstances.

Both improvement notices and emergency prohibition notices can be served on the Crown. These should be served on the appropriate Secretary of State and copied to the relevant solicitor for the department. A copy should be sent to the person in charge of the premises. Emergency prohibition orders may also be sought from the court. However, a prohibition order is not available, since a prerequisite for such an order is a conviction for breach of one of the Food Regulations.

CHAPTER FOUR:

EVIDENTIAL AND GENERAL PROCEDURAL MATTERS

Introduction

If a defendant is prosecuted for a criminal offence under the Food Safety Act, or under the Food Hygiene (General) Regulations 1970, or any other relevant enactment, the rules of criminal evidence will apply. These rules are the same whether the prosecution takes place in a Magistrates' Court or in a Crown Court. Here are some of the principles of the law of evidence relevant to food law prosecutions:

- Any person who is suspected of a criminal offence, and who is being questioned about it by an investigator, is protected by the provisions of the Police and Criminal Evidence Act 1984 and by the Codes of Practice made under that Act. If his rights have been infringed, any confession made by him may be excluded by the court. EHOs are in the same position as the police so far as observance of these safeguards is concerned.

- Any person who is being questioned about an alleged (or suspected) criminal offence is entitled to exercise his right of silence, and no adverse inferences can be drawn from any refusal to answer questions. There is one exception to this rule, namely where an accusation is made by a person who is on equal terms with the suspect: for example, a customer accusing a shopkeeper of selling bad food.

- It is not possible (except in the rarest of circumstances) for an EHO to repeat in a criminal court anything that he was told by an absent witness if the purpose is to rely on the truth of what was said. If a witness is unavailable or unwilling to give evidence at the trial, it may be possible to produce a written statement made by that witness instead. The appropriate provisions are to be found in sections 23 and 24 of the Criminal Justice Act 1988, and, in the case of computer records, in s.69 of the Police and Criminal Evidence Act 1984. These statutory provisions only permit documentary hearsay not oral hearsay, and even here there are safeguards for the defendant.

- Children are able to give evidence in criminal proceedings, even if they are too young to take an oath or give evidence on affirmation. The position is governed by s.33A of the Criminal Justice Act 1988, which states that the evidence of a child under the age of 14 must be given "unsworn". There is no minimum age for giving evidence in criminal proceedings and it is for the judge (or the magistrates) to decide the competence of a child as a witness. Arguments are unlikely to arise about this matter unless the witness is very young (less than 8 years old).

- Criminal Courts require the prosecution to prove each disputed allegation of fact "beyond reasonable doubt", unless Parliament has required the defendant to prove "due diligence" (as in the Food Safety Act) or some other relevant defence. In such a case the defendant has to prove his defence on the "balance of probabilities".

Appeals against Notices and Orders

Some doubt exists whether appeals against improvement notices and prohibition orders are civil or criminal proceedings. The same doubt exists regarding an application by an EHO under s.12 of the Food Safety Act for an emergency prohibition order. If, as a matter of law, appeals and s.12 applications are considered as civil rather than as criminal proceedings, the Criminal Justice Act 1988 will not apply. Accordingly, the EHO should bear in mind that he may not be able to rely on documentary statements from absent witnesses in such situations.

Some Working Definitions of Types of Evidence

It is useful to look at some definitions used by lawyers and textbook writers when discussing evidential matters.

Evidence   This may loosely be described as the facts and circumstances which might be used to establish the issues in dispute. As a general rule, questions of law (including Acts of Parliament) do not have to be proved as matters of evidence. The job of the advocate is to draw the court's attention to the rule of law in question, and to argue his interpretation of it. The same principle does not, however, apply to secondary legislation, such as statutory instruments or by-laws, or to "quasi-legislation" such as codes of practice or circulars.

Relevant Evidence   This is bound up with another term: "admissible evidence". The general rule is that all relevant evidence is admissible. Relevant does not have its ordinary meaning, but instead means legally relevant . Some evidence is relevant as a matter of common sense, but that does not make it legally relevant. An example of this is where a shopkeeper has a very bad record in food hygiene cases. A person might well take this record into account when deciding whether to shop there, but a court is not entitled to infer guilt from that record because it is not legally relevant.

Prima Facie Evidence   This is evidence which tends to show that the allegation made against the defendant may be true. In criminal cases, the defendant will be entitled to succeed in a submission of "no case to answer" if the prosecution fails to establish a prima facie case.

Direct Evidence   This is a term commonly used to describe evidence given by a witness of some fact in issue (or some circumstantial fact) which he has personally experienced. It is contrasted with an experience of another person which has been communicated to that witness, who then wishes to tell the court about it.

Circumstantial Evidence   This is evidence which is not itself direct evidence of a fact in issue in the case, but evidence from which a fact in issue may be inferred.

For example, in **Ward v Tesco Stores** [1976] the Court of Appeal held that the fact that a customer slipped on some yoghurt on the floor was circumstantial evidence of negligence.

Secondary Evidence   This is any evidence which is a substitute for something better (for example, a photocopy of a document). The modern approach is to treat secondary evidence as admissible evidence. However, a photocopy will not be any more admissible than a hand-written copy of the contents of the document. In the case of documents proper (e.g. contracts, leases, letters, invoices, books of account, and so on) the courts will not accept secondary evidence of their contents unless:-

1) a statutory provision permits this; or
2) evidence is given to show that the original document cannot be produced; or
3) the other party refuses (after notice) to produce the original document which is in his possession.

If copies are to be produced, the party doing so may rely on s.27 of the Criminal Justice Act 1988. This section permits copies of documents to be adduced and authenticated in such manner as the court may approve; and it states that "it is immaterial... how many removes there are between a copy and the original".

Hearsay Evidence   The rule against hearsay may be stated as follows: "an assertion, other than one made by a person while giving oral evidence in the proceedings, is inadmissible as evidence of any fact asserted." Hearsay therefore consists of three elements:

1) an assertion of fact;
2) a communication of that assertion to the court at some later time; and
3) a purpose in making that communication to the court (i.e. to prove the truth of the assertion).

The rationale for the rule is that the absence of the original witness renders inoperable the normal method of challenging the credibility of that witness, namely cross-examination. Therefore, even if the evidence relates to a very simple statement, not likely to have been misunderstood by any witness overhearing it, the rule against the admissibility of that statement still stands.

Even if the statement is in writing, and can be produced by a witness who has kept it safe and unaltered, the general rule against its admissibility still applies. This is why it is sometimes important to persuade a court that such things as tickets, labels, boxes, wrappers, and packages are not documents at all but material objects - or "real evidence", not covered by the hearsay rule.

If a statement (written or oral) is brought to the attention of the court - not for the purpose of proving that the contents of that statement are true, but merely to show that the document in question exists, or that the statement in question was made - the hearsay rule is not infringed. For example, if the defendant in a food safety prosecution is relying upon the due diligence defence, it may be permissible for the prosecution to call evidence of the fact that the same defendant was given a written warning about the same type of occurrence on one or more previous occasions. Even if the defendant denies that those warnings were justified, the prosecution can legitimately argue that he was put on his guard against permitting such infringements to occur in the future. For these purposes, it will not matter if the EHO who wrote the original warning letter is no longer available to give evidence, provided a copy of the letter exists and can be authenticated if necessary. There are important exceptions to the hearsay rule which are referred to below.

Real Evidence This consists of the production of material objects for inspection in court. Real evidence can be used to prove facts in issue, such as the presence of foreign bodies in food. Automatic recordings - such as computer printouts, video and audio tapes - are items of real evidence when tendered to show what it was that was recorded.

Documentary Evidence A document is sometimes merely an item of real evidence, i.e. something which can be produced for the inspection of the court in the same way as a physical object, such as the label on a packet of groceries (showing the "sell by" date or the name of the vendor). Usually, a document is produced because a party wishes to rely on it as evidence of the truth of its contents. Then it is known as documentary evidence.

Oral Evidence This is direct testimony of a witness, present in person and given on oath or affirmation. In the case of a child under 14 years old, the testimony is given in an unsworn and unaffirmed form.

The difference between oral evidence and documentary evidence is that in the former case the witness can be cross-examined in court; in the latter case, the evidence of the witness is encapsulated in a written document, audio tape, or video tape. Since the method of trial in common law jurisdictions places considerable emphasis on the examination and cross-examination of witnesses in court, documentary evidence is normally only admissible where statutory provision allows, such as the Criminal Justice Act 1988.

Avoiding the Hearsay Rule

Oral Hearsay
In criminal trials it is very difficult to avoid the rule against hearsay if the statement in question cannot be produced in a written form. If an EHO has interviewed a witness but without obtaining a written statement from him, it will be next to impossible for the EHO to give oral evidence of what he has been told should the witness subsequently refuse to come to court or be unable to do so, unless one of two exceptions applies. These exceptions arise when the EHO himself has been a witness to something very significant, for example when:

1)   a statement was made by a customer in the presence and hearing of the defendant, in circumstances where the defendant makes a reply to the accusation, or reacts in some significant way, or where the defendant's silence might be interpreted as a suspicious silence; or

2) a statement was made by a customer, or employee or some other relevant person, in circumstances where the common law dispenses with the hearsay rule because of the obvious spontaneity of the words used.

This last exception is known as the "res gestae" rule. It applies to various situations, most of them of an unusual or startling nature. For example, in **Manchester Brewery v Coombs** (1901) a witness was allowed to repeat what customers had said immediately after tasting and rejecting some beer.

Technically there is a further exception. A confession may be admissible even if unwritten, but the practical effect of the Code of Practice C, made under the Police and Criminal Evidence Act 1984, is to impose a requirement for a written statement in such situations.

Documentary Hearsay

If a statement has been put into writing, it may be admissible in criminal proceedings even though the maker of that statement cannot be called as a witness, if one of the grounds in s.23 or s.24 of the Criminal Justice Act 1988 applies. Section 23 states that a "statement made by a person in a document" is admissible in criminal proceedings where:-

1) the person who made the statement is dead or, by reason of his bodily or mental condition, unfit to attend as a witness; or
2) the person who made the statement is outside the United Kingdom and it is not reasonably practicable to secure his attendance; or
3) all reasonable steps have been taken to find the person who made the statement, but he cannot be found; or
4) the statement was made to a police officer (or some other person charged with the duty of investigating offences and charging offenders) and the person who made it does not give oral evidence "through fear" or because he is "kept out of the way".

The scope of "fear" in this context has not yet been clearly established by the courts. It may, for example, extend to non-physical causes, such as the fear of being sacked by an employer.

Business Documents

Section 24 of the Criminal Justice Act 1988 deals with business documents (documents "created or received by a person in the course of a trade, business, profession, or other occupation, or as the holder of a paid or unpaid office"). In the case of such documents, it is not necessary to show that the original maker of the statement himself made, signed, or otherwise created the document. It is only necessary to show that (whoever actually "created" the document) the information contained in it was "supplied" by a person who had, or who might reasonably be supposed to have had, personal knowledge of the matters dealt with in the statement.

It is also permissible for the information to have been indirectly supplied to the maker of the document, provided that each person through whom it was supplied received it in the course of a trade, business, profession, or other occupation, or as the holder of a paid or unpaid office.

So far as business documents are concerned there are a number of possibilities which will satisfy section 24:-

- the document may have been created (in the course of a trade, business, etc.) by a person who had personal knowledge of the facts recorded in that document; or

- the document may have been created (in the course of a trade, business, etc.) by a person who directly received the information from another person (not necessarily acting in the course of a trade, business etc.) who had personal knowledge of the facts recorded in that document; or

- the document may have been created (in the course of trade, business, etc.) by a person who indirectly received the information from someone with personal knowledge, through one or more intermediaries, each of whom was receiving the information in the course of a trade, business, etc. (not necessarily the same trade or business in each case).

Trade Documents and Investigatory Documents

However many people may have been involved in the creation of a business document, the Criminal Justice Act 1988 recognises two broad categories of such documents:-

1) Business documents created in the ordinary course of trade, business etc. Invoices, receipts, letters, books of account, accident reports, and similar Business documents fall within this category.
2) Business documents prepared for the purpose of "pending or contemplated proceedings", or for the purpose of a criminal investigation. The notebooks of an EHO, a trading standards officer, a police officer, or similar investigator fall within this category.

The difference between these categories is that the first type of business document would be created or received in exactly the same way whether or not a crime was subsequently suspected. Such documents may be of particular use in establishing the supply line of contaminated food. The second type of business document gives rise to the risk that it has been influenced (in its terminology or contents) by the fact that it is being created or received by a person who is conducting a criminal investigation, and who may be launching the very proceedings in which the document will be used.

Use of Business Documents in Proceedings

For the above reason, business documents which fall within the second category can only be used as evidence, under s.24 Criminal Justice Act 1988, in the following circumstances:-

1) where one or more of the conditions stated in s.23 have been satisfied (e.g. that the witness is too ill to come to court, and/or cannot be brought back from outside the U.K.); or
2) the person who made the statement cannot reasonably be expected (having regard to the time which has elapsed since he made the statement, and to all the circumstances) to have any recollection of the matters dealt with in the statement.

Whenever a document is prepared for the purposes of a criminal prosecution or investigation (even if it is not a business document), it will be necessary to obtain the leave of the court to make use of that document under s.26 Criminal Justice Act 1988. The prosecution will have to show that it is in the interests of justice that leave should be granted, having regard to the contents of the statement, the disadvantage caused to the opposing party by his inability to cross-examine the maker of the statement, and any other relevant circumstances. In any event, the court has a discretion to exclude documentary hearsay under s.28(1)(b) Criminal Justice Act 1988. For this reason, even if the document is an ordinary business document (e.g. an item of business correspondence) it will be advisable for the party seeking to make use of it to explain to the court why the maker of that document is not being called as a witness.

Electronic and Mechanical Printouts
It is possible to argue that some documents produced mechanically or electronically are not documentary hearsay but a form of real evidence. Much will depend on the purpose for which the document is being used. It is advisable to assume that the court might accept a submission by the defence that any form of mechanical or electronic printout is a document (including such things as a receipt produced by an automatic till roll).

In these circumstances, it will be necessary not only to lay the foundation for the admissibility of the document under s.23 or s.24 of the 1988 Act, but also to comply with the requirements of s.69 of the Police and Criminal Evidence Act 1984. This section states that a statement in a document produced by a computer (a word which is broadly defined) shall not be admissible as evidence of any fact stated unless it is shown:

1) that there are no reasonable grounds for believing that the statement is inaccurate because of improper use of the computer; and
2) that at all material times, the computer was operating properly, or, if it was not, that any respect in which it was not operating properly, or was out of operation, was not such as to affect the production of the document or the accuracy of its contents.

These matters can be established by producing a statement in the form of a certificate from any person occupying a responsible position in relation to the computer; it is sufficient if that person states these facts to the best of his knowledge. For the EHO, this means obtaining a written statement from the supervisor in charge of the equipment.

Witnesses

Witnesses may be divided into witnesses of fact and witnesses of opinion. The general rule is that the courts will only allow the parties to call witnesses of fact. Nevertheless, there are many common situations where ordinary people give opinions: about the time of day, the age of a particular person, or the size or weight of things seen or felt. Usually, there is no objection to witnesses of fact giving opinions on such matters.

Expert Witnesses

Where the answer to a question depends upon some form of technical or special knowledge only an expert witness may give an opinion. An expert must be wary about giving an opinion on anything outside his special knowledge or expertise. It is for the court to decide whether any witness is to be treated as an expert. If an EHO wishes to be called as an expert witness, he must first inform the court of his qualifications and experience.

Once a witness has been accepted by the court as an expert witness, he will be entitled to fortify his own opinion by reference to scientific works and other published sources of information that are commonly consulted by members of his profession. He will not, however, be able to give detailed evidence about particular experiments and tests which he has not himself carried out.

Evidence-in-Chief

A witness in court is not allowed to read out his proof of evidence. However, he may refresh his memory by reading it immediately before entering the witness box. The fact that he has done so will not affect the admissibility of his evidence, but it may influence the weight the court is prepared to give to it and the opposing side's lawyer should be told that this has occurred.

A witness such as an EHO - whilst giving his evidence - may ask for permission to refresh his memory from his notebook, or from any other record which was made at the same time as the events in question, or shortly after. The opposing party has the right to see this notebook (or other document) and will be at liberty to cross-examine the witness on its contents. It is wise, therefore, to seal up any parts of a notebook which do not relate to the evidence being given.

A witness is not allowed to read his evidence from a prepared statement; he is expected to give evidence in his own words, without being led by the advocate conducting the examination-in-chief. This means that the advocate cannot ask his witness leading questions, except in relation to those parts of the evidence that are not in dispute. A leading question is one capable of suggesting to a sympathetic, lazy, or forgetful witness the answer which the questioner is seeking to obtain.

Cross-Examination

The purposes of a cross-examination are to:-

- elicit further evidence;

- confront and, if possible, undermine the evidence-in-chief; and
- discredit the witness.

When cross-examination is aimed at the second purpose it is known as "cross-examination as to issue"; when aimed at the third, as "cross-examination as to credit". The defendant in a criminal trial has a special protection against cross-examination as to credit. This protection (or "shield") applies to food safety prosecutions in the same way as in other criminal proceedings. It is given to the defendant by s.1 of the Criminal Evidence Act 1898.

One aspect of this "shield" is the well-known rule that a defendant cannot be cross-examined about his previous criminal convictions. In food safety prosecutions, it will not usually be possible to refer to previous infringements simply to show that the defendant (whether an individual or a company) has a habit of breaking the law. This protection, however, may be lost in a few situations listed in s.1(f) of the 1898 Act. One of these is where the defendant makes assertions against the character of the prosecutor or a prosecution witness. In this situation the prosecutor can seek the leave of the court that the defendant has lost his "shield". Where leave is given, a defendant can then be questioned about his own bad character.

The rule against leading questions does not apply to a cross-examination.

Re-Examination
The purpose of re-examination is to deal with any fresh issues raised in cross-examination. It should not be used (although it sometimes is) for eliciting information which could have been given during the examination-in-chief. The rule against asking leading questions of one's own witnesses still applies, though it is less strenuously enforced in re-examination than in examination-in-chief. If the re-examination does raise new issues, the cross-examining party can apply for leave to conduct a further cross-examination of the witness.

Gathering the Evidence for a Prosecution
It is now possible to look at some particular problems in food safety prosecutions and to see how the rules of evidence should be complied with.

Taking Photographs
Any photographs going in as evidence should be agreed with the defendant's lawyers before the hearing. They may refuse to agree to any photographs which, intentionally or otherwise, give the impression that the defendant has committed offences other than those with which he is charged. It is therefore better to confine each photograph to a particular item, covered by a single charge, with no other infringements being depicted. For the same reason it is not advisable to put labels or annotations on a photograph, but simply to give them a number for identification purposes.

If the defendant's lawyers will not agree to the admissibility of a photograph, it will be necessary to produce a statement from the processor of the film that he printed the photograph from an unretouched negative. One way to avoid this requirement is to use a Polaroid camera, so that there will be one original set of photographs available for inspection by the court. Additional sets can be made from an inter-negative, or on a high quality photocopier. It is desirable to have one set of photographs available for each magistrate, as well as for the defendant's lawyers and the witness.

Witness Statements
A witness statement may be submitted to the court if the defendant (or his lawyer) has been served with a copy under s.9 of the Criminal Justice Act 1967 and has not objected to the admissibility of that statement. If an objection is made, the witness will have to be called to give oral testimony, unless the statement is admissible under s.23 or s.24 of the Criminal Justice Act 1988. Even if it is admissible under either of these sections, the leave of the court will be required before the statement can be used, because it is a document prepared for the purposes of a criminal prosecution.

Children and Mentally Handicapped Persons
If a child or a mentally handicapped person is being interviewed, the safeguards of the Police and Criminal Evidence Act 1984 (and the Codes of Practice made under that Act) will apply to that interview, whether the person being interviewed is a suspect or not. In short, this means that the interview should take place only in the presence of an "independent adult" (usually a parent in the case of a child being interviewed).

Directors and Proprietors
If an employee of a company or other enterprise is being interviewed, and the EHO has no intention of prosecuting that person, there will be no need to caution him before commencing the interview. He will simply be a witness, not a suspected person. Unless he is a child or a mentally handicapped person, the Police and Criminal Evidence Act will not be relevant.

If the person being interviewed is a proprietor of the business, or a director of the company, or a senior employee of any type of enterprise, different considerations apply. He may be at risk of being personally prosecuted; or he may be identified as an agent of his employer, authorised to make admissions about food safety matters; or he may be sufficiently senior to be part of the "brains" of the company rather than its "hands". In any of these situations, he should be cautioned so that he is made aware that he (and the enterprise which he represents) has a right of silence. There will be no need to caution if the EHO has decided not to use any answers given at the interview against the person in question, his employer, or the company he represents.

When to Caution
Paragraph 10.1 of Code of Practice C (made under PACE 1984) states that a caution must be given if there are grounds to suspect that the person being questioned has committed an offence. There is no obligation to caution a person being questioned merely as a witness. Therefore it is not obligatory to caution

during the ordinary course of sampling food or inspecting premises, or when the EHO is seeking to obtain information for possible use against third parties.

If during an interview the person being questioned makes an admission of guilt, or gives an answer which arouses suspicions of guilt, it will then be necessary for the EHO to give the caution as set out in paragraph 10.4 of Code of Practice C: "You do not have to say anything unless you wish to do so, but what you say may be given in evidence."

A distinction must be drawn between statements giving rise to a suspicion of guilt (or which contain admissions not previously suspected) and statements which confirm or reinforce a suspicion that was already there. The former statements (coming, as they do, by surprise) are admissible against the person being interviewed, even though no previous caution was given. The latter statements are not admissible, unless they were made or repeated after a caution had been given.

These requirements about cautioning apply to interviews taking place informally, or conducted by an exchange of letters, or carried out by telephone or fax, no less than to interviews conducted formally with contemporaneous notes.

The Right of Silence
Paragraph 11.4 of Code of Practice C states that a police officer or other investigator shall, without delay, cease to question any suspected person who makes it clear that he has nothing further to say. The silence of a suspected person cannot be used as evidence of guilt. What is less well known is that the prosecution cannot give further evidence of the questions which they put to him (or wanted to put to him) once he has decided to rely on the right of silence. This restriction applies to EHOs in the same way as it applies to the police.

Previous Warnings and Previous Convictions
The general rule is that it is not permissible to give evidence of a defendant's previous convictions (still less of his bad character) when seeking to prove him guilty of a criminal offence. If the defendant is relying on the due diligence defence, however, it may be relevant to adduce evidence of previous warnings which he (or his company) was given in the recent past. The previous warnings must relate to alleged infringements that were identical (or very similar) to those currently charged. These go to show that he was on notice as to the existence of a particular problem and the adequacy (or otherwise) of his response. If the warnings (or improvement notices) related to infringements of a different nature, it would be too prejudicial to allow such allegations of bad character to be used.

On Conviction
Once a defendant is convicted or has pleaded guilty, the rule prohibiting character evidence ceases to apply and his previous convictions can be brought to the attention of the court, together with details of relevant improvement notices and formal warnings. This is to assist the court in deciding the appropriate penalty.

There is an important restriction on the use to which previous convictions can be put. Spent convictions under the Rehabilitation of Offenders Act 1974 should not form part of the record for sentencing purposes. In practice, for food safety offences, this will mean that convictions more than 5 years old should be disregarded.

The controversial section 29 of the Criminal Justice Act 1991, which sought to limit the court's ability to take into account a criminal record as an aggravating factor in sentencing, is being repealed. It is not, therefore, being considered further in this book.

When considering the defendant's history of non-compliance with food safety legislation, EHOs should note that public limited companies and private companies do not become different persons in the eyes of the law merely because the directors or senior employees have changed since previous proceedings, or since any formal warnings were given.

Pleas in Mitigation

It sometimes happens that a defendant who has pleaded guilty afterwards makes (or instructs his advocate to make) a plea in mitigation asserting statements of fact which the EHO knows to be untrue. The EHO should have previously instructed the prosecuting solicitor on the facts of the case. In any event, the prosecuting solicitor (or EHO, if acting as advocate in the case) is entitled to tell the court that the facts alleged by the defendant are disputed by the prosecution. The court will then insist on the defendant giving evidence on oath and must allow the prosecution to call the EHO, or some other witness, to give evidence. Both witnesses may be cross-examined on their evidence. This type of sentencing hearing is known as a "Newton hearing".

Costs

In the event of a successful prosecution the prosecutor is entitled to ask for costs. Guidelines, issued by the Lord Chief Justice in 1991, make it clear that a prosecuting authority is not entitled to ask for costs to cover general overheads when carrying out its statutory duty to investigate offences. However, if special costs are incurred in an investigation (e.g. the costs of scientific tests or of photographs) these may be recovered from the defendant. Likewise, the general costs of devoting officers' time to the case, once the decision to prosecute has been taken, are recoverable. It should be borne in mind that the award of costs is discretionary and that the practice between courts will vary.

STATUTES, REGULATIONS AND CASES

Statutes

Criminal Evidence Act 1898, 30
Criminal Justice Act 1967, 31
Criminal Justice Act 1988, 22, 24, 26-28, 31
Criminal Justice Act 1991, 33
Food Act 1984, 5, 8
Food Safety Act 1990, 1, 3-8, 11, 14, 16, 18-21, 22
Local Government Act 1972, 5
Police and Criminal Evidence Act 1984, 2, 22, 26, 28, 31-32
Rehabilitation of Offenders Act 1974, 33

Regulations

Fresh Meat Export (Hygiene and Inspection) Regulations 1987, 16
Food Hygiene (General) Regulations 1970, 5, 9, 21, 22
Food Safety (Prescribed Forms) Regulations 1991, 13, 17
Food Safety (Sampling and Qualifications) Regulations 1990, 13

Cases

Manchester Brewery v Coombs (1901) 2 Ch 608, 26
Ward v Tesco Stores Ltd. (1976) 1 All ER 219, 24
Zawadski v Sleigh (1975), RTR 113, 8